D0604005

GOLDFISH

Danuta Wong

Grolier
an imprint of
◧ SCHOLASTIC
www.scholastic.com/librarypublishing

Published 2009 by Grolier
An Imprint of Scholastic Library Publishing
Old Sherman Turnpike
Danbury, Connecticut 06816

For The Brown Reference Group plc
Project Editor: Jolyon Goddard
Picture Researcher: Clare Newman
Designer: Sarah Williams
Managing Editor: Tim Harris

Volume ISBN-13: 978-0-7172-8043-8
Volume ISBN-10: 0-7172-8043-8

**Library of Congress
Cataloging-in-Publication Data**

Nature's children. Set 5.
   p. cm.
  Includes index.
  ISBN 13: 978-0-7172-8084-1
  ISBN 10: 0-7172-8084-5 (set)
  1. Animals--Encyclopedias, Juvenile. I.
Grolier Educational (Firm)
   QL49.N386 2009
   590.3--dc22
                            2008014674

Printed and bound in China

Contents

FACT FILE: Goldfish

Class	Ray-finned fish (Actinopterygii)
Order	Cypriniformes
Family	Carp and other fish (Cyprinidae)
Genus	Crucian carp, Japanese crucian carp, Prussian carp, and goldfish (*Carassius*)
Species	Goldfish (*Carassius auratus*)
World distribution	Goldfish originally come from China; now found worldwide as pets, and as pests when released into the wild
Habitat	Freshwater ponds and home aquariums
Distinctive physical characteristics	The common goldfish is gold or yellow with a streamlined body; fancy varieties have flowing fins, a rounded body, bulging eyes, and come in many different colors
Habits	Hearty feeders; breed after one year old; peaceful; can live more than ten years
Diet	Tiny water animals and aquatic plants

Introduction

Goldfish are among the most popular pets in the world. There are many different kinds of goldfish. These range from the common goldfish to round-bodied varieties with bubbly bumps on their head, bulging eyes, long, flowing **fins**, or even missing fins! These fancy fish come in orange, white, black, or some mix of those colors.

With the proper care, all types of goldfish can make great pets. They can live up to 10 years or more in an indoor **aquarium** or outdoor pond. With enough space, they might grow to more than 1 foot (30 cm) long.

Lionheads have head growths and no top fin.

Goldfish are a different species from their ancestors, the crucian carp.

History

Goldfish originated in China more than 1,000 years ago. People who kept a type of fish called the crucian carp for food noticed that some were more orange than others. By pairing the brightest orange fish to produce young over several generations, they developed the common goldfish. That kind of pairing is called **selective breeding**.

These pet fish spread to Japan. The Japanese then began to produce different varieties of goldfish about 500 years ago. In the 1700s, goldfish arrived in Europe, where they became popular. The craze for goldfish reached the United States in the mid-1800s. Not long after, goldfish farms were breeding American fish. Since that time, goldfish have been one of the most popular pets in North America.

Fishy Features

A common goldfish's streamlined body can cut through water with ease. The fish propels itself by swishing its tail from side to side. The paired fins on the lower sides of the body steer the fish as it swims. The single fins above and below help with balance. To move up and down in the water, the fish has a balloonlike part called a **swim bladder** inside it. To rise, this hollow **organ** fills with air. To sink, the air comes out of the bladder.

Most of a goldfish's body is covered in **scales**. These see-through, small plates are outgrowths of the fish's skin. They overlap—like the tiles on a roof. This arrangement allows water to flow smoothly over the fish's body as it swims, enhancing its streamlined shape. Scales also help protect the fish's skin.

Fish are cold-blooded animals. Their body temperature changes with the temperature of their surroundings.

9

Goldfish can get bored just like people. They like the company of other goldfish. A group of goldfish is sometimes called a "troubling."

Breathing in Water

Animals that live on land, such as lizards, cats, and humans, need oxygen to survive. These animals have lungs, which take oxygen from the air. Fish need oxygen to survive, too. Instead of lungs, they use **gills**. The gills are in their head. The goldfish's gills are covered and protected by a tough flap called a gill cover.

To breathe, water continually enters the fish's mouth. The water passes over the gills. The gills are made up of very many fine fingerlike parts called **filaments**. Together, the filaments provide a large surface area for oxygen from the water to pass into the fish's blood inside the filaments. The bloodstream then carries the oxygen all around the body.

Goldfish Senses

To find food, escape danger, and recognize members of their own species, goldfish need to have good senses. They have good color vision, but they are nearsighted. That means they have to swim close to something to get a good look at it. Goldfish also have to view objects from the side because they cannot see that well in front of themselves.

Goldfish use their senses of smell and taste to find food in the water. Dirty water can affect a goldfish's sense of smell, making it harder for it to locate food. Although goldfish do not have any externals ears like cats, dogs, and humans, they do have inner ears in their head to hear underwater sounds. In addition, goldfish have nerves along the sides of their body that detect vibrations in the water. These nerves—called the **lateral line system**—channel the vibrations to the fish's brain, where it makes sense of them.

Fish owners should never "pet," or touch their fish. Goldfish have a protective slimy coat. Rubbing any part of this away can increase the risk of the fish becoming ill.

The coloring of the
black moor gives it
a velvety appearance.

Goldfish Galore

Fish can be divided into two main groups. Those that live in freshwater, such as ponds, rivers, and lakes, and those that live in the saltwater of the seas and oceans. A few types of fish, such as salmon, spend part of their life in freshwater and part in saltwater. Goldfish live in freshwater.

There are more than 100 varieties of goldfish. All are bred from the original common goldfish. Many breeds are gold, but there is also a wealth of other colors, including white, yellow (sometimes called lemon), bronze, red, chocolate, or a mixture of these colors. There are also goldfish that are totally black!

Goldfish also come in many shapes. Many varieties, such as the common goldfish, comet, and shubunkin, are shaped much like a typical fish. However, varieties have been bred with a round body, bulging eyes, a bubbly head, and very long, wavy fins. Although more difficult to care for, these fancy varieties can live a long time and make rewarding pets.

Picking a Pet

Healthy goldfish have clear eyes, rigid fins, and they are active swimmers. Clouded eyes, droopy fins, and poor swimming are all signs of illness. These fish are not likely to survive for long without expert medical care. If there are several dead fish in a tank in the pet store, don't buy any of the fish in that tank. There might be a serious health problem affecting all of the fish.

The staff in a pet store should be able to give you good advice about goldfish. First-time fish owners should feel free to ask a lot of questions. They should avoid buying fancy breeds until they have some experience. If buying more than one goldfish, it is best to get all of the same variety. Some varieties are better swimmers than others. The best swimmers are likely to take over less active varieties in the tank. They will also take the lion's share of the food!

Goldfish fascinate
people of all ages.

Shubunkins' scales
are a mixture of
pearly and metallic.

For Beginners

Common goldfish, comets, and shubunkins are all ideal goldfish for the first-time owner. These varieties are hardy and easy to care for.

The common goldfish is bright orange from head to tail. It is similar in shape—streamlined with a short tail—to its carp **ancestors**. Common goldfish can live to longer than 10 years, grow to more than 12 inches (30 cm), and weigh up to 6½ pounds (3 kg).

The comet looks similar to the common goldfish, but it has a much longer, deeply forked tail. It was first bred in the United States not long after goldfish first arrived there. Like common goldfish, comets can grow to 12 inches (30 cm). They come in various colors.

Shubunkins are probably the toughest breed of goldfish. These strong swimmers need a big tank. They can live a long time—up to 20 years—and grow to 16 inches (40 cm). They have longer fins than common goldfish, and their coloring is called **calico**—mainly white with yellow, gold, red, and black spots and patches.

Fancy Fish

Popular fancy varieties of goldfish include fantails, orandas, and telescope eyes. Most of these kinds of fish can grow to 8 inches (20 cm) long from nose to tail.

Fantails have a double tail with streaming fins that look like a lady's fan. They are usually orange or white. For a fancy variety, they are relatively tough. They survive equally well in an indoor aquarium or an outdoor pond. Orandas have a head growth that looks like a raspberry. These fish do not survive well outdoors. They need to live in water kept at a constant 65°F (18°C), so they are best kept indoors. Telescope eyes have bulging eyes. Again, these varieties are best kept in an indoor tank. Black telescope eyes are called black moors. There is even a black-and-white variety known as the panda moor!

The growth on
an oranda's head
is called a wen.

Lionheads were
first bred in China.

Poor Swimmers

Although fancy varieties of goldfish look elegant, many are poor swimmers. These varieties include lionheads, pompoms, and celestials. These fish should never be mixed in a tank with more active varieties of goldfish. If they are, they will get knocked around and be the last to reach the food at feeding time.

Lionheads are also called tomatoheads. They have a lionlike "mane" of blisters around their head. The mane can be yellow or gold. Lionheads do not have a top, or **dorsal**, fin. Pompoms have two flowerlike growths on the end of their nose. Like lionheads, some pompoms do not have a dorsal fin.

Unusual eyes are common in the more exotic varieties of goldfish. Celestials have eyes that point upward. Unfortunately, these fish cannot see in front of themselves at all!

Setting Up

Taking on any type of pet requires commitment and knowledge about the animal. Before buying any pet, a would-be owner needs to learn about the animal, how to take care of it, how much it will cost to buy and look after, and how long it will probably live. It is a good idea to read a book from the pet store or library on the care of goldfish before getting one as a pet. In addition, there are many web sites that give information on caring for goldfish.

If you are sure that you have the time to care for and maintain a goldfish tank, the next step is to buy the right equipment and one or more fish. A good pet store should have all the equipment you'll need, the right kind of food for goldfish, and several varieties of fish to choose from. The staff in a pet store should be able to advise you about which type of goldfish to get, how to set up your tank, and how many fish it can hold.

Room to Move

A goldfish's home should be bought and set up before buying the fish. The bigger a goldfish's tank is, the better. Goldfish need much more space to move around in than a fishbowl can provide. Small goldfish bowls should never be a permanent home for a fish. They are generally too small for active fish and do not provide enough surface area—where the water meets the air. Surface area is very important because the bigger it is, the more oxygen from the air can get into the water.

Fish need a lot of room. They grow quickly and can soon outgrow a small or medium-sized tank. In addition, goldfish produce a lot of waste. In a small tank, the poisons from the waste soon build up and cause health problems for the fish. For four goldfish, a 20-gallon (76-l) tank is recommended as a healthy size. That's fairly big for small fish—but they will soon grow.

Goldfish are not completely covered in scales—their head and fins do not have scales.

Equipment

A first-time goldfish owner will need to buy more than just a tank for the fish. The tank will need a cover, or hood. The hood allows air to get in, but keeps dust from falling in and the fish from leaping out. The hood may also be fitted with a light. Fluorescent lights are best because they do not heat the water, which will make it uncomfortable for the fish. Goldfish thrive best at water temperatures of 46 to 64°F (8 to 18°C).

The tank should be equipped with a **filter**. The filter keeps the water clean by removing dirt and waste. The pet store should be able to recommend the right kind of filter for your tank. You should also ask for an **aerator**. This machine blows bubbles into the water, increasing the amount of oxygen. Aerators also help get rid of the waste gas carbon dioxide.

Bubbles increase the amount of oxygen in the water.

For every inch (2.5 cm) of goldfish, there should be at least one square foot (930 sq cm) of surface area in a tank.

Prime Location

An aquarium needs daylight, but not direct sunlight. In bright sunlight, the water will become too warm. Warm water holds less oxygen than cold water. Bright sunlight also encourages the growth of small plantlike living things called **algae**. A little algae is good for the fish, but a lot can cloud the water and dirty the walls of the aquarium.

The aquarium will also need to stand on a strong table or base. A 20-gallon (76-l) tank will weigh about 200 pounds (90 kg).

The bottom of the tank should be lined with gravel. About 40 pounds (18 kg) will nicely cover a 20-gallon (76-l) tank. Gravel can be bought from a pet store. Rinse it thoroughly first to wash out any chemicals or dirt that may be in it. Once the gravel is in place, the next step is to add water.

Adding Water

The best way to add water to an aquarium is to pour it in very gently. That way, the gravel will not be churned up. When the tank is full, add plants. Pet stores sell both live water plants and artificial ones. Simply push the roots of the live plants into the gravel. They will soon become established. Plants are helpful because they produce oxygen, they use some of the goldfish's waste to grow, and goldfish like to nibble on them.

Add ornaments and artificial plants next. Then place the aerator and filter in the water. Make sure you follow their directions carefully. Finally, switch on the filter and aerator and leave them running for 48 hours. This time period allows the filter to clean the water and also allows for any chemicals, such as chlorine, to **evaporate**. You might want to buy a water-testing kit from the pet store. The kit will show you if the water still contains chemicals that might harm fish. If all's well, the tank is now ready for fish.

If tank water is not filtered, a buildup of wastes, such as feces and carbon dioxide from the gills, can soon reach levels that poison a fish.

A newly bought goldfish should not be kept in a small bag for very long. Goldfish need oxygen and room to move.

A New Home

Goldfish usually come home in clear plastic bags. Never pour your new fish from the bag into the aquarium as soon as you get it home. That can be too much of a shock for the fish. A goldfish needs time to adjust to the temperature and water of its new home. The best way to ease the transition is to float the bag containing the fish in the tank. Within 15 minutes, the temperature of the water in the bag and in the tank should be the same.

Next, add some tank water into the goldfish's bag. That will help the fish adjust to the water in its new home. The water from the pet store and the water in an aquarium will be different. After another 15 minutes, it is safe to gently pour out the fish into the tank. Once released, the curious fish can explore the new home.

Varied Diet

In the wild, goldfish eat insect **larvae**, **aquatic** worms and crustaceans, other tiny animals in the water, and plants. Goldfish food from pet stores usually comes in the form of dry flakes or pellets. Soaking the food in tank water before feeding it to the fish makes it easier for fish to **digest** the food. Pet stores also sell freeze-dried insects and shrimp, which goldfish especially like. Some pet stores even stock live food, such as worms and insect larvae. To vary their diet even more, you can give goldfish shredded boiled peas and lettuce. Goldfish will also nose around in the gravel for morsels to eat.

Goldfish should be fed twice a day, once in the morning and once in the evening. Try to keep a regular feeding schedule. Do not give too much food. Their mealtimes should not last more than two minutes—otherwise they will keep eating and eating.

Goldfish have toothlike structures in their throat that help them crush their food.

Always keep an eye on a cat
if it is in the same room as
an aquarium. Cats are natural
hunters and will try to scoop
goldfish out of the water.

Maintenance

If you have a fish tank, you will need to perform a few tasks daily, weekly, or at longer intervals to make sure it is in perfect working order and clean.

Each day, look at the filter and aerator to make sure they are both working. Check that the water temperature stays within 46 to 64°F (8 to 18°C). Switch off the tank light at night. Goldfish do sleep!

Once a week, remove any parts of the plants that have turned brown and uneaten food lying on the gravel surface. Also remove up to a third of the water in the tank. That keeps the levels of wastes in the water that the filter cannot remove low. Replace the water with water that has been kept separate for a few days in a large container. Give your fish a weekly health check, too. Cloudy eyes, a swollen body, sluggish or unbalanced swimming are all signs that a fish needs medical attention.

Once a month, scrape off the algae growing on the tank's walls. Remove dirt from the filter and aerator and clean any ornaments. Every three months, rinse out or replace the filter. Finally, every six months, empty the tank and clean it out.

Staying Healthy

Goldfish commonly suffer from illnesses caused by **fungi** and **parasites**. These living things feed off the fish and affect their health. Patches of fungi look like miniature cotton balls. There are various types of parasites that can live on or in fish. Flukes live in the fish's gills, making them red and swollen. Anchor worms burrow under a goldfish's scales, causing wounds. Fish lice look like small disks and can attach anywhere on the outside of a fish.

If one fish in a tank has any of these problems, it is best to treat all the fish. That's because fungi and parasites can spread easily among fish. A vet or the staff at a pet store can give you medications that will soon rid the fish of these pests.

Healthy fins are free from damage and spread or fan out in the water. Fins that are droopy, frayed, or with parts missing are signs of a disease called fin rot.

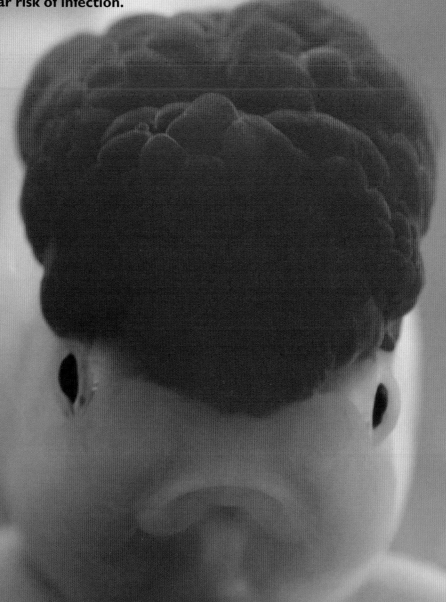

The wen, or head growth, of fancy varieties, such as this oranda, are at particular risk of infection.

Problems

Some foods do not agree with certain types of goldfish. They can cause a blockage in the fish's **digestive tract**—a condition called **constipation**. Slim breeds of goldfish, such as the veiltail, are especially at risk from constipation if given dry food. Constipated fish appear swollen and tend to lie on the bottom of the aquarium. Such a fish should be separated from others. The fish should not be fed for a few days until it becomes more active. Its diet then needs to be changed, for example to freeze-dried food. After a week, return it to the main tank—but make sure it no longer eats dried food.

Fish that cannot balance properly or swim upside down usually have problems with their swim bladder. Pet stores stock special food that can treat this problem.

Some goldfish develop unsightly bumps, or growths, on their body. These usually can be removed safely by a vet.

The Great Outdoors

Several varieties of goldfish survive well in outdoor ponds. They include common goldfish, comets, shubunkins, and fantails. Goldfish can be mixed with another type of ornamental carp called koi (KOY). These fish are a different species. Like goldfish, koi come in many different colors. They have whiskerlike feelers, called **barbels**, below their mouth. Koi generally live longer than goldfish—up to 60 years.

Some people move their fish indoors in winter. However, many types of goldfish can survive winter outdoors. During the cold months, they become sluggish and do not eat.

With more room,
fish in ponds tend
to grow bigger than
those in aquariums.

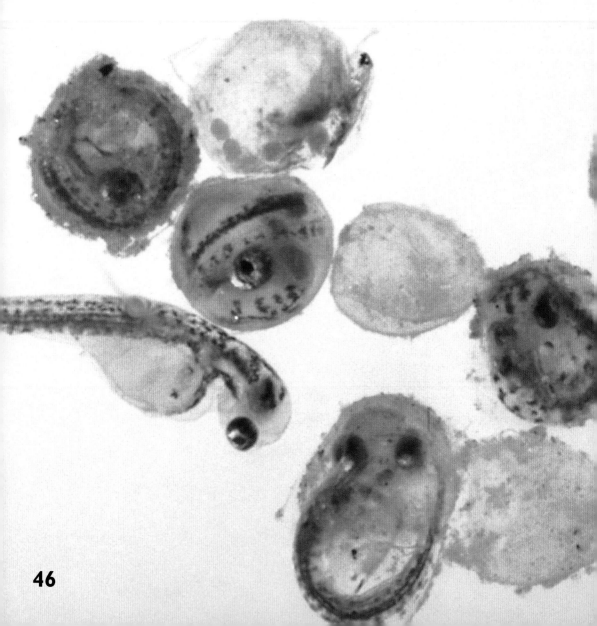

After hatching,
goldfish fry remain
by their eggshell.
They eat a store
of food inside it.

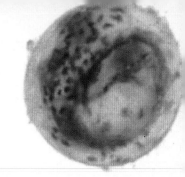

Breeding Time

Indoor goldfish can **breed** anytime of the year.
Outdoors, breeding takes place in the summer.
Male and female goldfish usually look the same,
but in the breeding season they show differences.
The females become fatter, and males develop
small pimples called tubercles on the sides of
their head and front fins. They also chase the
females around the tank or pond. Eventually,
the females release thousands of tiny eggs. The
eggs stick to plants. The male goldfish release
a substance called milt, which **fertilizes** the
eggs. Inside the eggs, baby fish develop. After
about five days, the eggs hatch. Young fish
are called **fry**.

Some goldfish breeders give their fish
special food before the breeding season. They
also separate the fish they want to breed into
special breeding tanks.

Growing Up

Goldfish are terrible parents—not only do they not look after their young, they will eat them! For that reason, fry and adult goldfish are kept in separate tanks. Pet stores sell special food for fry. When they are a couple of weeks old, they can be fed live crustaceans called daphnia, or water fleas.

In a few weeks, the fry are looking more fishlike. They are greenish brown in color. In ponds, that color is helpful. It allows them to blend into their background so that larger **predatory** fish will not see them. Outdoors, young fish usually hide among water plants around the edge of the pond.

At about a year old, the young fish begin showing their colors. With luck, this new generation of goldfish will live to ten years or more in a large tank or pond.

Words to Know

Aerator   A machine that blows air bubbles into an aquarium.

Algae   Tiny, green plantlike living things that live in water and moist places.

Ancestors   The early types of an animal.

Aquarium   A glass tank filled with water that houses fish.

Aquatic   Living in water.

Barbels   Whiskerlike feelers near the mouth of certain types of fish.

Breed   To produce young.

Calico   A blotched or spotted pattern.

Constipation   A condition where there is a blockage in the digestive tract.

Digest   To break down food in the body.

Digestive tract The body parts involved in eating and getting nutrients from food. The mouth, stomach, and intestines are all parts of the digestive system.

Dorsal   On the back of an animal.

Evaporate   When a liquid is changed into vapor.

Fertilizes   When fish eggs and milt mix. The eggs can then develop into new fish.

Filaments	Tiny fingerlike parts of the gills.
Filter	A machine that cleans water by removing dirt and wastes.
Fins	Thin, flat extensions of a fish's body, used for moving, steering, and balancing in water.
Fry	Young fish.
Fungi	Types of living things that include molds, yeasts, and mushrooms.
Gills	The breathing organs of fish.
Larvae	The young forms of insects.
Lateral line system	Nerves on the sides of a goldfish's body that detect vibrations in water.
Organ	A part of the body with a specific function, such as a heart or gill.
Parasites	Animals that live on or in other animals.
Predatory	Like a predator—an animal that hunts other animals for food.
Scales	Overlapping, see-through plates that form a protective covering on a fish.
Selective breeding	Choosing which animals can have young together to produce certain characteristics, such as size and color.
Swim bladder	A balloonlike sac inside a fish. Fish inflate it to rise in water and deflate it to sink.

Find Out More

Books

Barnes, J. *Pet Goldfish*. Pet Pals. Milwaukee, Wisconsin: Gareth Stevens Publishing, 2006.

Johnson, E. L., and R. E. Hess. *Fancy Goldfish: Complete Guide to Care and Collecting*. Boston, Massachusetts: Weatherhill, 2001.

Web sites

Animal-World: Goldfish Varieties
animal-world.com/encyclo/fresh/goldfish/Goldfish.htm
A lot of information about goldfish varieties.

Goldfish Types
www.kokosgoldfish.com/ftypes.html
More facts and pictures of different goldfish varieties.

Index